On the Move

PLANES

Ursula Pang

PowerKiDS press

PK Beginners

Planes can fly!

Planes have wings.
Wings help a plane
go up and down.

WINGS

Some planes have propellers. Propellers make the plane go!

PROPELLER

Some planes have
jet engines.
Jet engines make the
plane go too!

JET ENGINE

All planes need a pilot. The pilot drives the plane.

PILOT

Large planes have two pilots.
The second pilot is called the copilot.

PILOT
COPILOT

Pilots work
in the cockpit.

EXTERIOR LIGHTS
PASS WARN
COCKPIT LIGHTS
ANTI ICE HTR
WINDSHIELD HEAT
EMER LDG GEAR
FUEL CONTROL

Small planes can only carry a few people.

CAUTION!
CAUTION!

The biggest planes can carry lots of people!

Fighter planes are the fastest planes!

Have you ever been on a plane?

Published in 2025 by The Rosen Publishing Group, Inc.
2544 Clinton Street, Buffalo, NY 14224

First Edition

Editor: Greg Roza
Book Design: Rachel Rising

Photo Credits: Cover, p. 1 best images/Shutterstock.com; p. 3 Denis Belitsky/Shutterstock.com; p. 5 muratart/Shutterstock.com; pp. 7, 9 frank_peters/Shutterstock.com; p. 11 Doglikehorse/Shutterstock.com; p. 13 Skycolors/Shutterstock.com; p. 15 Alexander Tolstykh/Shutterstock.com; p. 17 Geewon Jung/Shutterstock.com; p. 19 Matej Kastelic/Shutterstock.com; p. 21 Eliyahu Yosef Parypa/Shutterstock.com; p. 23 Quality Stock Arts/Shutterstock.com.

Library of Congress Cataloging-in-Publication Data

Names: Pang, Ursula, author.
Title: Planes / Ursula Pang.
Description: Buffalo : PowerKids Press, (2025) | Series: On the move
Identifiers: LCCN 2023051479 (print) | LCCN 2023051480 (ebook) | ISBN 9781499444667 (library binding) | ISBN 9781499444650 (paperback) | ISBN 9781499444674 (ebook)
Subjects: LCSH: Airplanes--Juvenile literature.
Classification: LCC TL547 .P265 2025 (print) | LCC TL547 (ebook) | DDC 629.133/34--dc23/eng/20231107
LC record available at https://lccn.loc.gov/2023051479
LC ebook record available at https://lccn.loc.gov/2023051480

Manufactured in the United States of America

CPSIA Compliance Information: Batch #CSPK25. For further information contact Rosen Publishing at 1-800-237-9932.